California
First-Year
Law Students'
Examination

Essay Questions
and
Selected Answers

October 2014

October 2014

ESSAY QUESTIONS

California First-Year Law Students' Examination

Answer all 4 questions.

Your answer should demonstrate your ability to analyze the facts in the question, to tell the difference between material facts and immaterial facts, and to discern the points of law and fact upon which the case turns. Your answer should show that you know and understand the pertinent principles and theories of law, their qualifications and limitations, and their relationships to each other.

Your answer should evidence your ability to apply the law to the given facts and to reason in a logical, lawyer-like manner from the premises you adopt to a sound conclusion. Do not merely show that you remember legal principles. Instead, try to demonstrate your proficiency in using and applying them.

If your answer contains only a statement of your conclusions, you will receive little credit. State fully the reasons that support your conclusions, and discuss all points thoroughly.

Your answer should be complete, but you should not volunteer information or discuss legal doctrines that are not pertinent to the solution of the problem.

You should answer according to legal theories and principles of general application.

The State Bar Of California
Committee of Bar Examiners/ Office of Admissions

180 Howard Street • San Francisco, CA 94105-1639 • (415) 538-2300
845 South Figueroa Street • Los Angeles, CA 90017-2515 • (213) 765-1500

ESSAY QUESTIONS AND SELECTED ANSWERS

OCTOBER 2014

CALIFORNIA FIRST-YEAR LAW STUDENTS' EXAMINATION

This publication contains the four essay questions from the October 2014 California First- Year Law Students' Examination and two selected answers for each question.

The answers were assigned high grades and were written by applicants who passed the examination. The answers were produced as submitted by the applicant, except that minor corrections in spelling and punctuation were made for ease in reading. They are reproduced here with the consent of the authors.

Question Number	Subject
1.	Contracts
2.	Torts
3.	Criminal Law
4.	Contracts

QUESTION 1

Zena placed an advertisement in a local newspaper: "Wanted: Someone to clean my four-bedroom, four-bath house (2500 square feet) once a week for the next month; pay $35 per hour. No interview or references necessary. The first to apply will be accepted." She included her phone number.

Carl called her the next day and said, "I accept on the terms you have offered." Zena said, "You should know there was a mistake in the advertisement. The pay will be the same, but my house is actually 3000 square feet."

Carl said, "Let me think a moment."

Zena replied, "I have a call on another line, and I'll call you right back." When she called Carl two minutes later, Carl said, "I agree to clean for you on the terms you described. An extra 500 square feet does not matter to me."

Zena told Carl, "I'm sorry, but I've changed my mind and I think I'll do my own cleaning."

Carl sues Zena for breach of contract.

Is Zena liable to Carl? Discuss.

QUESTION 1: SELECTED ANSWER A

Is Zena liable for Carl?

Zena (Z) v. Carl (C)

Contract

For a contract to be valid there must be an offer, acceptance, consideration, and no formation defenses.

Governing Law

The Uniform Commercial Code (UCC) governs contracts that are for the sale of goods.

Service contracts are covered under common law, not the UCC. Here the contract is for a cleaning service and therefore this contract is governed by common law.

Offer

An offer is an objective present contractual intent communicated to the offeree with clear and definite terms.

Under common law the terms required for a contract are quantity, time for performance, identification of the parties, price and subject matter.

Advertisement

An advertisement is generally not considered an offer. However if the advertisement has clear and definite terms such that the advertisement may meet the requirements for an offer, some courts will allow for an advertisement to be considered an offer.

When Z placed an ad in the paper her terms were:

quantity - my house

time for performance - Once a week for a month

parties - first to apply

price - $35 per hour

subject matter - cleaning

Because Z's advertisement in the paper has clear and definite terms her advertisement would likely be viewed as an offer.

Acceptance

Assent to the terms of the offer.

When C stated that, "I accept on the terms you have offered" C assented to the terms and showed an outward manifestation to be bound by the contract.

Z may argue that because her advertisement stated, "The first to apply will be accepted" and C stated that he accepted, C did not properly accept the contract. However a reasonable person would look at the conduct and what was said and likely find that acceptance was appropriate.

Modes of Acceptance (Mailbox Rule)

The offeror is the "master of the offer" and may specify a specific mode of acceptance. If the offeror does not, acceptance is done by a reasonable method given the method of the offer. Additionally, an acceptance is effective upon dispatch and a rejection is effective upon receipt.

Z included her phone number in the advertisement. This shows Z's intent that reasonable acceptance may be done by phone. C called Z the day after the advertisement was placed.

Timely Response

It is reasonable to assume that the following day after an advertisement goes into the paper when C called, that the acceptance is reasonably timely.

Mirror Image Rule

Under common law, an acceptance had to be a mirror image of the offer (additional or different terms would likely be a counteroffer or if asked properly an inquiry).

Consideration

Consideration is a bargained-for exchange/legal detriment.

Z was not bound to pay C for cleaning the house; the $35 per hour is a bargained-for exchange and a legal detriment. C was not previously bound or had a preexisting duty to clean Z's house. There is valid consideration for both parties.

Contract Formed

As discussed supra, there was a valid offer, acceptance and consideration. Absent a formation defense, a contract has been formed.

Formation Defense, No offer

Z will argue that the advertisement was not an offer. However for the reasons discussed supra, she will not win on this argument.

Formation Defense, Mistake

If there is a mutual mistake that goes to the heart of the bargain, the contract may be rescinded by the harmed party.

In the facts given there is no mutual mistake as a slight increase in the square footage of the home is not likely significant.

Unilateral Mistake

When there is a unilateral mistake to a contract, the contract may be unenforceable if it is unconscionable, or the non-mistaken party knew of or should have known of the mistake.

Z will state that she made a mistake in the offer and therefore she should be let out of the contract. However the contract on its face is not unconscionable, nor could C have known of the mistake.

Z will not prevail on this argument.

Statute of Frauds

Contracts for the sale of goods, in consideration of marriage, surety, sale of real property, and contracts that cannot be completed within a year are required to be in writing. Here there are no facts to support the statute of frauds is an issue as the contract is for a month's time.

Modification

A contract may be modified under common law so long as there is additional consideration and both parties assent to the modification.

When Z stated her house was actually 3000 sq feet and the pay was the same, Z attempted to modify the contract.

Additional Consideration for Modification

Consideration defined supra.

Because there was additional cleaning to be done 500 sq feet C would have more cleaning to do. Additional work would be legal consideration. C is being paid by the hour ($35). Because cleaning additional areas would take longer, C would be paid more.

Therefore this modification would have consideration.

Assent to Modification

When Z told C that she wanted to modify the contract, C said, "Let me think a moment". Let me think is not an outward appearance to agree to the modification and therefore C is not bound to the modification at this point.

When Z called C back C stated, "I agree to clean for you on the terms you described. An extra 500 sq ft does not matter to me." C assented to the modification and the modification therefore became valid.

Timeliness and Mode of Acceptance of Modification
Defined supra.

Z stated she had another call and would call C right back. Upon calling C right back, C accepted the modification. Therefore the mode and timeliness of the acceptance of the modification were valid.

The modification of the contract is valid for the reasons discussed supra.

Revocation of an Offer
An offer may be terminated by communicating to the offeree prior to acceptance.

Z will argue that she terminated the offer when she stated she changed her mind and would do her own cleaning. Because the offer had already been accepted (discussed supra) Z cannot terminate the offer.

Breach
A breach occurs when one side to a contract does not perform. A breach may be major (goes to the heart of the contract) or may be minor.

Anticipatory Repudiation

When a party to a contract states clearly (through words or actions) they will not perform under the contract, the other party may treat the repudiation as a breach.

When Z stated she changed her mind, Z effectively said she was not going to perform under the contract. Because cleaning the house was the heart of the contract, this would be seen as a major breach.

C would be excused from his promise to clean.

Good Faith

A party to a contract may not make performance impossible and enforce the contract. Therefore Z does not have a claim of breach.

Expectation Damages

A party to a contract is entitled to the benefit he would have received had the contract been performed.

Here C would be entitled to $35 times the number of hours it would have taken to clean the house (as the modified contract stated) minus any expenses he would have had in cleaning the house.

Call 1. Is Zena liable to Carl?

For the reasons discussed supra, yes Zena is liable.

QUESTION 1: SELECTED ANSWER B

Carl v Zena

Governing Law

The Common Law governs contracts for services, as the Uniform Commercial Code governs contracts made for the sale of moveable goods.

The facts state the contract is for house cleaning, a type of service.

Thus the Common Law will be the governing law.

First Offer

An offer is a present outward manifestation of contractual intent, with clear and definite terms, communicated to the offeree.

Advertisement

According to Majority Rule an advertisement is merely a proposal for offers.

Minority Rule states if the Advertisement contains clear and definite terms could be an offer.

Here the facts indicate that Zena places an advertisement in a local newspaper for house cleaning services, showing a manifestation of present contractual intent, as she described the service needed.

The advertisement also included the following terms:
Quantity: 1

> Time of performance: Once a week/next month
>
> Identity of parties: Zena and 1st to apply
>
> Price: $35 per hour
>
> Subject matter: 4 bedroom house (2500 sq ft)

Since the terms are clear and definite, and stated with particularity they become part of the offer.

Also, because Zena placed her phone number in the advertisement, and received a call from Carl, it was communicated to the offeree.

Because all the terms are clear and definite if the courts follow the minority rule they will construe this advertisement to be an offer.

If the courts decide it is merely an invitation for offers, and follow the Majority rule, it will not be a valid offer.

Reasonable Person - Objective Theory of Contracts

According to the objective theory of contracts, the most reasonable person would view Zena's offer in the newspaper as an offer, because all the terms are clearly stated, and it states the first person to apply will be accepted. Also a reasonable person would see Zena's phone number, not just merely an ad, and would believe that she could be contacted immediately to accept the cleaning service.

Acceptance #1

An acceptance is an unequivocal assent to the terms of the offer.

Here, Carl calls Zena the next day, stating, "I accept on the terms you have offered," showing an unequivocal assent to the terms of the offer, made using her telephone number, a call assenting to the "<u>master of the offer</u>," <u>to return</u> an acceptance in phone call. If the courts find there was a valid offer, then Carl's acceptance will also be valid.

Zena will argue that because she received the phone call from Carl, their conversation also included that she made a mistake in the advertisement which she stated before the conversation was over.

As will be discussed below, if the courts decide that Zena does have a valid point then the offer will be terminated; if not, then Carl will have made a valid acceptance.

Termination – Oral Conversation.

Because an oral conversation has taken place between Carl and Zena, and Zena made a statement of making a mistake in her advertisement, at the end of the conversation, Carl states "Let me think about it," we can infer that there was no decision made.

Thus the oral conversation terminates the offer, since no decisions were made.

Exception Unilateral

A unilateral contract cannot be terminated once performance has begun. Here, because Carl and Zena have not made a decision, or agreed upon one, and no performance has begun the offer is still terminated at the end of their conversation.

OFFER #2

Offer defined supra.

During Carl and Zena's phone conversation, Zena proposed a mistake in her first offer to Carl. She stated that the pay will be the same, but my house is actually 3,000 square feet, in which implies different terms, thus creating a second offer to Carl.

Acceptance #2

Because Zena hung up the phone, and called Carl two minutes later, Carl then stated an unequivocal assent to the terms of her second offer.

Thus a valid acceptance.

Revocation

An offeror may revoke their offer anytime prior to a timely acceptance. Revocation is effective upon receipt.

Here, the facts indicate after Carl accepts Zena's offer, Zena then tells Carl, "I'm sorry, but I've changed my mind," indicating a revocation of her offer to Carl.

Since Zena's revocation was not prior to the acceptance by Carl, it will not be effective.

Thus not a valid revocation.

Meeting of the Minds/Mistake

The courts will view the contract by both Zena and Carl to be mutual if they show that they knew of the contract, and a reasonable person would believe that they were entering this contract with no doubts.

Zena will argue that there was no meeting of the minds because she made a mistake in her advertisement, and when Carl called they hung up, and two minutes later before Zena could respond, Carl is stating that he accepts the terms. This is not giving her enough time to respond or react to the second offer; he just came out and said I agree to your terms.

Thus if the courts side with Zena and there was no meeting of the minds then there will be no contract, if they side with Carl a contract has been formed.

MISTAKE – UNILATERAL

Usually the courts will side with the non-mistaken party and go by what they state was in the contract at the beginning of formation.

Carl will argue that Zena made a mistake in her advertisement, clearing it up with him later, and he still accepted her new terms.

Thus the court will side with Carl and use the terms of the contract that were formed during formation.

Consideration

Consideration is a bargain for exchange of a legal detriment.

Here, Zena is bargaining for her house to be cleaned, and Carl is receiving $35 per hour to clean her home.

Thus a bargain for exchange has been made.

Thus a valid contract exists.

Defenses to Formation
Mistake – Unilateral

As discussed above, Zena created a unilateral mistake, but fixed the mistake with Carl after the advertisement was posted.

Thus not a valid defense.

STATUTE OF FRAUDS

Statute of frauds requires some contracts to be in writing: Marriage, debt of another, contracts that cannot be performed within one year, $500.00 or more, and interest in land.

Because this contract is for house cleaning services it does not fall within the statute of frauds.

Thus not a valid defense.

BREACH

Major Breach – Here because Carl did not receive his benefit of the bargain, Zena has created a major breach of contract.

Remedies

Reformation

Due to the mistake that Zena made in her advertisement, which was later cleared up, Carl may ask the courts to reform the contract to what both parties intended it to be at the time of formation.

Rescission

Due to Zena's unilateral mistake she may ask the court to rescind the contract, and apply the agreed upon terms.

QUESTION 2

Homer and Wanda are husband and wife. The furnace in their home stopped working. Wanda wanted to call a licensed repair person, but Homer insisted on attempting to fix it himself, despite having no knowledge of how the furnace worked.

After working on the furnace for some time, Homer informed Wanda that he had fixed it. Wanda and Homer then went out to dinner. When they arrived home, they found that it had been destroyed by fire. They were informed by a firefighter at the scene that the fire appeared to have originated in the furnace. When Wanda started yelling at Homer for "burning the house down," Homer slapped her to calm her down.

Wanda sued Homer for negligence and battery. At a jury trial, she presented evidence proving the facts stated above. At the close of evidence, Homer moved for a directed verdict on the following grounds:

1. Spouses cannot sue each other in tort;

2. Wanda failed to present sufficient evidence to support a finding that Homer was negligent; and

3. Homer is not subject to liability for slapping Wanda because his intent was to calm her down, not to cause her any harm.

How is the judge likely to rule on Homer's motion for directed verdict? Discuss.

QUESTION 2: SELECTED ANSWER A

WILL HOMER'S MOTION FOR DIRECTED VERDICT SUCCEED?

IDENTIFICATION OF THE PARTIES: Homer is the defendant; Wanda is the plaintiff.

STANDING TO SUE:

I. CAN SPOUSES SUE EACH OTHER IN TORT?

According to common law, spousal suits against each other were not generally allowed. However, the current trend is to allow suits between spouses especially when intentional torts are involved. Thus, whether Wanda can sue Homer would essentially be a jurisdictional issue and a matter of law which the judge would determine. If the judge rules that no, spouses cannot sue in tort, Homer's liability will terminate and the directed verdict will be granted. However, this is unlikely considering the current trends allowing suits between spouses. Here, we will assume that spouses are allowed to sue each other in tort of both intentional tort and negligence.

II. IS HOMER NEGLIGENT?

Here, the question of negligence would relate to the burning of the house and whether Homer's actions were sufficiently negligent in causing the burning. Negligence requires the finding of a duty imposed upon the Plaintiff (Homer), a breach of that duty, causation of the injury and an actual injury.

1. DID HOMER HAVE A DUTY?

Duties are usually evaluated according to a reasonable person standard unless a special relationship exists between the parties. The reasonable duty of care is generally the duty to not harm another person and to act in a reasonable manner designed not to place others in unreasonable harm.

IS THERE A SPECIAL DUTY VIA RELATIONSHIP?

Here, the parties are husband and wife. A duty of care between husband and wife, as immediate family, is higher than the duty imposed regarding an average unrelated citizen. The duty to protect from harm is greater because of the relationship between Homer and Wanda. Because the duty to not harm Wanda is greater than the reasonable person standard a duty can be assignable to Homer.

2. DID HOMER BREACH THAT DUTY?

A breach of duty requires actions be committed by the Plaintiff (Homer) that place others in unreasonable danger or heightened risk. Breach can be established via statute (negligence per se) where a violation of civil or criminal statute imposes automatic fault (which then, if the violation is a civil statute, constitutes a rebuttable presumption by the Plaintiff). Here, there is no negligence per se because there is no mention of a statute being violated. Breach can also be established through clear explicit facts and/or the definable overt actions of the Plaintiff (Homer). However, the facts here are murky. Thus, a third method of determining breach must be used--the method of res ipsa loquitor.

Res ipsa loquitor allows an inference of breach when clear facts supporting breach do not exist. Res ipsa requires that the defendant be in clear control of the instrumentality that caused the injury, that the injury would not have occurred without some sort of negligence by the defendant, that no possible superseding acts occur that would remove the defendant from the chain of control over the instrumentality, and that the plaintiff (Wanda) not have participated in their own injury.

RES IPSA LOQUITOR AS VEHICLE FOR FINDING BREACH OF DUTY

a. DID HOMER HAVE CLEAR CONTROL OVER THE FURNACE?

Here, the instrumentality that caused the injury (the destruction of the property, the "house") appears to be the "furnace in their home" that had "stopped working". It states that Homer "insist[ed] on attempting to fix it himself" instead of "call[ing] a licensed repair person". There is no mention of any other person or thing interacting with the furnace between the time Homer "attempt[ed] to fix it himself" and the "burning" of the house. This means Homer was ostensibly the last person to interact with the furnace and a reasonable person could conclude that Homer had a clear control over the physical object of the "furnace" which ostensibly caused the injury, "burning". This element is most likely met on its face since the "furnace" was within the purview of the "home" which would be interpreted to be under Homer's control (dominion).

b. WOULD THE INJURY HAVE OCCURRED WITHOUT SOME SORT OF NEGLIGENCE BY THE DEFENDANT?

This is a more sticky issue than the clear control issue, supra, which seems to be a straight physical-control-over-the-object question. This element focuses more on the interaction the defendant had on the object in question.

On first glance, it seems that since Homer "having no knowledge of how the furnace worked" but yet "attempting to fix it himself" would infer that his lack of experience likely caused improper repair on the furnace which then, according to the firefighter at the scene, seemed to be the cause of the fire that "appeared to have originated in the furnace". It appears on its face that Homer's repair led to the fire. However, could the furnace have posed a fire risk prior to Homer's repair efforts? Perhaps. Did Homer's repair in fact actually place the furnace in a condition that would cause a fire risk when his attempt at repair would not? This is unknown. The facts state that "the furnace in their home stopped working" but it doesn't state what stopped working or why. There is also no mention of a defect to the furnace prior to repair that would pose a fire risk.

Surface review would appear to assign Homer's actions as a direct cause of the fire. But, the fact that a firefighter (although ostensibly an expert in the field of fighting fires) making the statement that the fire "appeared" to have "originated in the furnace" is not a direct statement of "the furnace started the fire because it had been repaired incorrectly". This is probably a matter for an expert witness to determine at trial. If Homer's actions did not cause the fire because the furnace was already damaged and at a fire risk and Homer's "repairs" did not place that furnace in a higher state of unreasonable unsafety then the injury of "the burning of the house" may not be attributable to Homer's act of trying to fix the furnace and negate this element of res ipsa loquitor resulting in no negligence. However, if this element is met the other elements of negligence must also be met to find liability on the part of Homer.

c. WERE ANY ACTS OR EVENTS INTERVENING OR SUPERSEDING CAUSES OF THE INJURY THAT WOULD RELEASE DEFENDANT FROM LIABILITY?

Intervening and superseding acts are those outside occurences separate from the defendant's actions that may break the chain of causation within the res ipsa loquitor analysis. Intervening acts are those that occur that are foreseeable consequences of defendant's acts and do not relieve defendant of liability. Superseding acts are those that are outside the realm of foreseeability and would be those so out of the ordinary that they would relieve the defendant of liability. Intentional torts and criminal acts are considered superseding.

Here, we don't know what acts may or may have occurred between the "attempt[ed]...fix" by Homer and the "home...destroyed by fire" that may or may not have "originated in the furnace". As discussed above, the exact cause of the fire is only an assumption at this point, not a definitive statement of fact. Further analysis outside the fact pattern will be needed.

It is to be noted that the acts of the fire department in attempting to stop the fire may have contributed to the "destruction" of the home. However, acts done during attempts to rescue are foreseeable results of a "fire" by those public servants tasked with protecting the public, "firefighters". Even if actions by the fire department are found to be negligent that will not release Homer from any potential liability since intervening acts of negligence are always considered foreseeable.

d. DID PLAINTIFF CONTRIBUTE TO THEIR OWN INJURY?

It is unlikely Wanda will be considered to have contributed to her own injury, the "destruction" of the "house" by "fire". However, she did want to call a "licensed repair person" but was persuaded to let Homer fix the furnace instead despite the fact that she (likely) knew Homer had "no knowledge of how the furnace worked". Was this enough to place some responsibility of "destruction" of the "home" by "fire" on Wanda? Perhaps. Again, additional facts will be needed.

Assuming the elements of res ipsa loquitor are met, there will be a finding of breach on the part of Homer.

3. WAS THE BREACH THE CAUSE OF THE INJURY?

Again, as discussed above in the res ipsa loquitor section, whether Homer's breach in trying to "fix it [the furnace] himself, despite having no knowledge of how the furnace worked" caused the injury of "destruction of the house by fire" is uncertain. If breach is found via res ipsa loquitor then this element of causation will also be met since the question posed here will be answered in the analysis of res ipsa loquitor.

4. WAS THERE AN INJURY?

An injury here would be the destruction of the "house" by "fire" which would constitute property damage and thus qualify as "injury" for negligence. Pure economic damages are not recoverable but personal injury and property damages do qualify as "injury" for the purposes of negligence.

DEFENSES TO BREACH

Homer may have several defenses to breach that would negate his liability and thus allow a directed verdict. The only two potential defenses are comparative negligence and assumption of risk. Comparative negligence jurisdictions allow a complete bar to plaintiff recovery if that plaintiff contributed in any manner to their own injury. As above, assignment of responsibility to Wanda will be necessary to trigger comparative negligence and bar her from recovery. A bar to recovery would allow a directed verdict for Homer regarding the negligence claim. Contributory negligence, while a defense more often available in a majority of jurisdictions, assigns risk to plaintiffs based on their percentage of fault and reduces their recovery accordingly. Here, only a finding of fault in excess of 50% on Wanda's behalf (in Pure Comparative Negligence jurisdictions) or 50% or higher (Modified Comparative Negligence jurisdictions) would bar her from complete recovery. Finding Wanda at fault in excess of 50% or 50% or higher is unlikely and thus comparative negligence in both its forms would only serve to reduce damages which would then prohibit Homer from receiving his directed verdict. Assumption of the risk is a defense that states a plaintiff is barred from recovery if they knew of the risk and voluntarily assumed it. Here, there is no clear assumption of the risk of "destruction of the home by fire" by Wanda and thus she did not voluntarily assume it. This is not a defense.

III. DID HOMER COMMIT A BATTERY AGAINST WANDA?

Battery is the intentional volitional act of the defendant against the plaintiff causing an offensive or harmful touching of the plaintiff's body or person (a connected object suffices). The reasonable person standard applies when evaluating what is "harmful" or "offensive" contact.

Here, the defendant "Homer" intentionally and volitionally "slapped [the plaintiff] [[Wanda] to calm her down" which would be considered a harmful and offensive touching of the body of "Wanda" when evaluated by a reasonable person. There is a battery because Homer intended to touch her and caused a harmful and offensive touching.

DEFENSES TO BATTERY

Homer poses a defense to battery that his intent was "to calm Wanda down" and not "cause her alarm". However, the reason behind the battery is not relevant, only the intent to touch and a resulting harmful or offensive contact is needed to establish battery. There is no defense to battery.

CONCLUSION: There is likely standing for the parties to sue; negligence on the part of Homer has not been clearly established with the facts at hand; Homer did commit a battery. There will be no directed verdict in favor of Homer.

QUESTION 2: SELECTED ANSWER B

WANDA v. HOMER

SPOUSAL IMMUNITY?

SPOUSAL IMMUNITY is where a husband and wife cannot sue each other. This theory is no longer observed in most modern jurisdictions, but is the common law.

The facts show that Wanda sued her husband. In common law a husband and wife could not sue each other. Modernly, this is no longer observed and spouses can, and do, sue each other.

If a common law jurisdiction, Wanda could not sue Homer.

NEGLIGENCE?

NEGLIGENCE is found where there is a DUTY owed, a STANDARD OF CARE to be followed, a BREACH of the DUTY, the BREACH is the ACTUAL CAUSE of plaintiff's injury, the PROXIMATE CAUSE of plaintiff's injury, and DAMAGES are suffered by plaintiff.

DUTY?

DUTY is the responsibility to not cause unreasonable risk of harm to others.

The facts show that Homer wanted to repair the furnace in their house. He had a duty to not unreasonably cause risk of harm to others in the house by doing so.

Homer owed a duty.

STANDARD OF CARE?

STANDARD OF CARE is the care that must be observed to ensure that defendant's actions are reasonable.

Homer's standard of care owed was to ensure that the furnace was repaired in a safe manner, so as not to burn the house down, or cause harm to his house or his wife.

Homer owed a standard of care to Wanda.

BREACH OF DUTY?

BREACH OF DUTY is failure to perform one's duty, supra.

The facts show that Homer did not know how to repair a furnace. He breached his duty because he wanted to fix it himself, despite having no knowledge of how to do so. This was a breach because he did not know how to fix a furnace.

Homer breached his duty.

RES IPSA LOQUITUR?

RES IPSA LOQUITUR finds that plaintiff has suffered an injury that is not normally found in the absence of negligence, plaintiff was not contributorily negligent, defendant had complete control of the item that caused the injury, and defendant in a better position to explain what happened.

After Homer fixed the furnace Homer and Wanda left the house and went out to dinner. Because nobody was home, the exact cause of the fire could not be determined without an expert's inspection of the premises. However, normally a house does not burn down right after a furnace has been worked on. Because the furnace work was done by someone who did not know how to work on furnaces, there is an appearance of negligence. Wanda was not contributorily negligent toward the house burning down because she did not work on the furnace. Homer had complete control of the furnace because he worked on it prior to the house burning down. Homer was in a better position to explain what caused the fire to start because he worked on the furnace.

Absent proof of actual breach of duty, supra, Wanda could rely on res ipsa loquitur.

ACTUAL CAUSE?

ACTUAL CAUSE is the event that ignites events that causes plaintiff's injury and is satisfied by the but-for or substantial factor test.

The facts show that after working for some time on the furnace, Homer believed that he had fixed it. This was the actual cause that ignited the event that burned their house down. But for Homer working on the furnace, the house would not have burnt down.

Homer was the actual cause of the injury.

PROXIMATE CAUSE?

PROXIMATE CAUSE is the foreseeable result of the actual cause, supra, unbroken by independent or superseding intervening events.

The facts show that after Homer worked on the furnace, the house burnt down. This was a foreseeable event of someone doing repairs on a furnace by someone who does not know how to work on a furnace. There were not intervening events because the firefighter informed them that the fire originated in the furnace.

Homer was the proximate cause of the injury.

CONTRIBUTORY NEGLIGENCE?

CONTRIBUTORY NEGLIGENCE is where plaintiff contributes to her own injury and is a complete bar to recovery. This theory has been abolished in most jurisdictions, but is still the common law theory.

The facts show that Wanda wanted to call a licensed repair person but let Homer work on the furnace himself. Wanda contributed to her own injury because she should have insisted that the professional furnace repair person be there. She was responsible for the house burning down because she didn't insist on a professional doing the repair.

Absent a valid defense, Wanda was contributorily negligent.

LAST CLEAR CHANCE?

LAST CLEAR CHANCE is a valid defense to contributory negligence supra, where plaintiff is found contributorily negligent but defendant had the last clear chance to avoid the injury.

The facts show that Wanda was contributorily negligent, supra. However, Homer had the last clear chance to avoid the injury by not working on the furnace when he had no knowledge on how to do so. Had he waited until a professional could work on the furnace, the house would not have burnt down.

Homer had the last clear chance to avoid the injury and Wanda's recovery is not barred.

COMPARATIVE NEGLIGENCE?

COMPARATIVE NEGLIGENCE is found where defendant is liable for the injury, plaintiff contributed to her own injury, and can recover damages in an amount apportioned to defendant's liability.

The facts show that Homer was liable for the injury because he worked on the furnace and the house burnt down. Wanda contributed to her own injury because she did not insist on a professional repairing the furnace. If the jurisdiction is a comparative negligence jurisdiction, she could recover damages in an amount apportioned to Homer's negligence in burning down their house.

There was comparative negligence.

STRICT LIABILITY?

STRICT LIABILITY is liability without fault where an abnormally or dangerous activity is found.

The facts show that Homer had no knowledge of how to work on a furnace. Because furnaces are dangerous pieces of equipment subject to exploding, this could be classified as an abnormally dangerous activity. Homer did not have the skill to work in this manner, and the fact that the house burnt down with the fire originating at the furnace shows that there was a dangerous element to this repair.

Homer may be strictly liable.

DAMAGES?

DAMAGES are required if plaintiff is to recover for negligence.

Wanda's house was burned down; therefore she suffered an injury. She could recover general damages for pain and suffering and special damages for the cost of the house that burnt down.

Wanda can recover damages.

BATTERY?

BATTERY is the intentional, harmful, offensive touching of another without consent or privilege.

The facts show that Homer slapped Wanda when she yelled at him for burning the house down. This was an intentional touching because he intended to slap her. It was a harmful touching because he did slap her. It was an offensive touching because slapping people is not acceptable adult behavior. Homer did not have Wanda's consent to slap her, nor did he have a privilege to slap his wife.

Homer argued that he was only trying to calm her down. However, this is offensive and harmful because it is not acceptable to slap people to calm them down.

Homer is liable for battery.

DAMAGES?

DAMAGES, supra.

Wanda could recover general and special damages, supra. She could also recover punitive damages for Homer's wanton and willful battery.

1. Homer's motion for directed verdict for spousal immunity should be granted if a common law jurisdiction.

2. Homer's motion for directed verdict for negligence should be denied because Homer was negligent.

3. Homer is liable for slapping Wanda because he committed intentional battery.

QUESTION 3

Steve and Frank became acquainted at a correctional facility for mentally ill violent offenders. Steve was an inmate who had to take antipsychotic medication to prevent paranoia. Frank was employed as a kitchen helper. Once they discovered that they both wanted to be actors, they hatched a scheme to kidnap a famous actor, Art, upon Steve's release from the facility, and to show him their acting skills. They believed that, once Art saw how talented they were, he would help them get acting jobs. They would then release him.

When Steve was released, he stopped taking his antipsychotic medication. As a result, he went in and out of paranoia. On bad days, he developed a belief that Frank had supernatural powers and that he had to do what Frank said or Frank would kill him. While Frank knew Steve was mentally ill, he was not aware of the severity of his illness.

Steve and Frank located Art's house, kidnapped him and took him to a remote location. During the kidnapping, Steve believed that Art was going with them willingly to assist them in their acting careers. After they arrived at the location, and while Frank was out, Steve beat Art and took his wallet. In a panic, Steve stole a car and drove away at a high rate of speed.

A police officer followed Steve and tried to stop him. Steve, believing the kidnapping, battery, and robbery had been discovered, attempted to escape by driving greatly in excess of the speed limit. During the high speed chase, the officer's car spun out of control and he died in the accident.

1. What charges, if any, can reasonably be brought against Frank for the beating of Art and the taking of his wallet? Discuss.

2. What charges, if any, can reasonably be brought against Frank for the death of the police officer? Discuss.

3. What defenses, if any, can Steve reasonably raise against a charge of kidnapping Art? Discuss.

QUESTION 3: SELECTED ANSWER A

State v. Frank for Battery and Robbery of Art

Accomplice Liability

At common law, all parties to a crime were labeled accessory before the fact, accessory after the fact, a primary or secondary accomplice. Here, both Steve and Frank are primary accomplices as they are effectuating the kidnapping. As such, they will be liable for all foreseeable crimes that occur during the perpetration of the kidnapping of Art.

Art would argue that the he did not participate in the battery or robbery of Art as he had left the location where Steve beat Art and he had only agreed to a kidnapping. This argument would fail because Frank knew Steve was mentally ill and was not in full control of his capacities. Frank left Steve alone with Art even though he wasn't sure of the extent of Frank's mental illness. The kidnapping was using force and it would be foreseeable that Steve would continue to use force to detain Art.

Frank would argue it wasn't foreseeable that physical force would be used after the kidnapping had occurred and they were sitting in a remote location. His intent was to get discovered as an actor not an intent on his part to steal Art's wallet.

Frank would lose as the continuation of kidnapping and the battery and larceny of the wallet that continued within the crime were foreseeable.

Conspiracy

At common law, conspiracy is an agreement between two or more people to commit an illegal act. Modernly, most jurisdictions require an overt act.

Steve and Frank hatched a scheme to kidnap an actor. The hatching is the agreement for the illegal purpose of kidnapping. In some states, simply agreeing to kidnap Art is the act needed, while in others the overt act was going to Art's house and actually kidnapping him. Under either view this crime is complete because they kidnapped Art from his home and took him to a remote location.

Under the Pinkerton Rule, once the conspiracy is formed, coconspirators are liable for all the actions of all their partners in furtherance of the conspiracy. Frank would argue that the beating and theft of the wallet were not in furtherance of the conspiracy, that the conspiracy was only kidnapping. However, the crime of kidnapping was continuing, they had not let Art free nor had Frank tried to withdraw so he is liable for all the criminal acts of Steve.

State v. Frank death of police officer

Accomplice liability supra

Conspiracy supra

Robbery

Is the trespassory taking and carrying away of the tangible personal property of another (trespassory taking is wrongful) with the intent to steal (permanently deprive) plus the use of force or threat of force. Here, Frank's co-conspirator beat (use of force) Art and took his wallet (tangible personal property) and left the remote location (carrying away).

Homicide

Is the death of a human being by defendant's acts.

Actual Cause

Requires but for the defendant's wrongful act, the officer would not have died. Here, had Frank not participated in this criminal venture with Steve, the police officer wouldn't have chased a scared Steve and died.

Proximate Cause

It is foreseeable that a police officer would die when engaged in a high speed chase.

Murder

Murder is a homicide committed with Malice.

Malice can be proven in one of four ways, intent to kill, intent to cause serious bodily injury, wanton & willful conduct and the felony murder rule.

Here, Steve Frank's liability would rest on the felony murder rule if the police officer died within the commission of an inherently dangerous felony. There is a split of jurisdictions on an inherently dangerous felony definition; some define it as the manner in which the felony is carried out and some define it by statute. Burglary, arson, robbery, rape and kidnapping all qualify as felony murders. Frank would argue that this death would not fall within the felony murder rule because the officer's death occurred after Steve had left his place of apparent safety and abandoned the kidnapping. This argument would fail because Steve was speeding away from the police thinking that the kidnapping, robbery and battery had been discovered. Steve was still in the commission of his criminal acts, which Frank shared accomplice liability for.

If the court found that the Felony murder rule did not apply, then the death of the officer would be determined as a 2nd degree murder.

There are no defenses available to Frank.

Defenses of Steve

Steve would assert an insanity defense. Under the M'Naghten rule, a person is not liable for his criminal acts if he cannot understand either the nature or character of his acts.

The "right or wrong" test requires that the defendant due to mental disease or defect cannot cognitively realize that what he is doing is wrong. If an "irresistible impulse" jurisdiction the defendant would argue that he didn't have the volitional, physical capacity to control his behavior. The model penal code standard uses both of those tests combined. Finally, in the federal courts and one state, Steve could assert the "Durham" test which states that if the act is a product of his mental disease, he is not guilty by reason of insanity. Steve's history of mental illness in a correctional facility, the medications he takes for the illness, the effect of paranoia in the majority jurisdiction of M'Naghten would mean Steve's mental disease of paranoia made it impossible for him to know what he was doing was wrong.

QUESTION 3: SELECTED ANSWER B

<u>State v. Frank</u>

<u>Solicitation</u>

Encouraging another to commit a crime with the intent they do it.

Here the facts do not clearly show who instigated the idea to kidnap Art. In any case this crime would <u>merge</u>, with Conspiracy and the target crime.

<u>Conspiracy</u>

Two or more persons agreeing to commit a crime. Modernly it requires an act in furtherance of the crime.

Here, Frank and Steve "hatched a scheme to kidnap ... Art." Kidnapping is a crime and they agreed to do it. They "located Art's house" – an act in furtherance of the kidnapping.

Frank is guilty of Conspiracy.

<u>Pinkerton's rule</u> – Accomplice liability

Under Pinkerton, all conspirators are responsible for all of the foreseeable crimes in furtherance of the conspiracy.

Frank will be guilty of all foreseeable crimes committed by Steve during the kidnapping.

<u>Battery</u>

Unlawful force to another.

Here, "Steve beat Art" during the kidnapping. Normally, battery of some sort occurs during and as part of a kidnapping and is a lesser included offense that <u>merges</u> <u>with</u> the kidnapping.

In this case, the battery was not incident to the kidnapping and may be charged separately.

Frank may be charged with battery as part of the kidnapping; however, if this battery was <u>not</u> a foreseeable part of the conspiracy, Frank will not be guilty of Frank beating Art.

<u>Larceny</u>

Trespassory taking and asportation of the property of another with the intent to permanently deprive.

Here, Steve "took Art's wallet;" since it was during Art's kidnapping, it would have been from his person, thus a 'trespassory taking.' Steve 'drove away' with the wallet, satisfying asportation. There is nothing to suggest he meant to return it at any time, since he fled "in a panic."

There is a larceny by Steve.

<u>Robbery</u>

Larceny (supra) by force or intimidation.

Steve's taking Art's wallet after beating him suggests the wallet was taken by force.

Steve committed Robbery.

As above, if these were the foreseeable consequences of the conspiracy, Frank will be charged with Robbery in the taking of Art's wallet.

Frank will argue the Battery and Robbery were not foreseeable; however the State will point out that these <u>are</u> foreseeable crimes and do occur in many kidnappings.

Frank will be charged for <u>all</u>, including the death of the police officer.

Murder

Homicide
One person causing the death of another.

Causation

Actual
But for Steve speeding away the officer wouldn't have died.

Proximate
It is foreseeable that an officer in pursuit at high speed could lose control of his car and die.

We have homicide.

Malice
May be shown in various ways.

Intent to kill/commit great bodily harm
Not evidenced in facts.

Felony Murder Rule (FMR)
Death during commission of an enumerated felony shows malice – Kidnapping (infra) is such a felony.

<u>Wanton and Reckless Conduct</u>

Driving at 'excessively high speeds' is wanton and reckless.

We have Malice.

<u>Murder in the First Degree (M1)</u>

May be shown in various ways, including

<u>FMR</u>

If death occurs during the enumerated felony – Kidnapping (infra) – M1 may be charged.

Here, Steve was attempting to escape pursuit from the scene of the kidnapping. He had <u>not</u> reached a place of safety; thus the officer died as a part of the kidnapping.

M1 may be charged.

If this fails:

<u>Murder in the Second Degree (M2)</u>

Death as a result of Wanton and Reckless disregard of life and safety may be charged as M2, which falls under all Murder that is not M1.

Here Steve "attempted to escape driving greatly in excess of the speed limit." This shows Depraved Heart because such action is likely to harm or kill someone.

If the court does not find Murder, the death of the officer would be:

<u>Voluntary Manslaughter (VM)</u>

Death due to criminal negligence.

Here in addition to the 'high speed,' Steve drove "in excess of the speed limit " – a statutory violation. Thus VM may be charged under <u>Misdemeanor Manslaughter</u> as well as Criminal Negligence.

Frank will be chargeable, as such flight and its consequences are the foreseeable result of the conspiracy (Pinkerton) (supra).

Kidnapping

Taking and moving another without Justification or Excuse.

Here the facts state that the kidnapping occurred as the result of the conspiratorial acts of Frank and Steve.

Defenses for Steve

Insanity

Steve will claim that he was not responsible for his actions.

M'Naughton

Steve will argue he could not understand what he was doing since "Steve believed that Art was going with them willingly."

Steve's illness doesn't meet M'Naughton though because "he went in and out of paranoia." Also, Steve knew what he had done since he "believed the kidnapping…had been discovered."

Irresistable Impulse

Steve's following Frank's direction may fall under this during a paranoid episode but will also fail.

<u>Model Penal Code</u>

As a blend of the above defenses, Steve's best defense is that due to his illness, he didn't have the necessary intent at the time of the kidnapping.

These will all likely fail as, when he was aware and fleeing, he didn't abandon the crimes.

QUESTION 4

Doug, a developer, and Bill, a builder, entered into a contract. Under the contract, Bill was to build a building for Doug for $100,000, and was to receive a $10,000 "on-time bonus" if he were to complete construction by a specified date.

Bill, in turn, entered into a contract with Ellen, an electrical contractor. Under this contract, Ellen was to do the electrical work for the building for $15,000. At the time she entered into the contract, Ellen was not aware of Bill's on-time bonus, but learned about it before she was to begin the job.

In the midst of the job, after receiving $3,000 in progress payments, Ellen decided she could not profitably do the electrical work for $15,000 and quit. Bill looked diligently for an electrical contractor to complete the work at the lowest cost. The only electrical contractor Bill could locate was Roger. Roger demanded $20,000 to complete the work. Bill agreed and paid Roger $20,000 upon completion.

In spite of Bill's best efforts, and solely because Ellen had quit the job, Bill completed construction late and, as a result, did not receive the on-time bonus.

1. Is Ellen liable to Doug for any damages Doug may have incurred as a result of the late completion of the construction? Discuss.

2. Is Ellen liable to Bill for:

   a. The loss of the on-time bonus? Discuss.

   b. For any other damages? Discuss.

QUESTION 4: SELECTED ANSWER A

1. IS ELLEN LIABLE TO DOUG FOR ANY DAMAGES DOUG MAY HAVE INCURRED AS A RESULT OF THE LATE COMPLETION OF THE CONSTRUCTION?

DOUG V. ELLEN

U.C.C./COMMON LAW

The common law governs contracts for the sale of goods. A good is tangible property that is moveable and identifiable at the time and of the formation of a contract.

In this case, the subject matter is the construction of a building. This is not a good, but rather Doug is bargaining for Bill's service and Bill is bargaining for Ellen and Roger's service.

Therefore, common law rules will govern this case.

FORMATION

An enforceable contract consists of a valid offer and a valid acceptance, together known as mutual assent, plus consideration, minus applicable defenses.

Facts state that a valid contract between Doug and Bill had been formed wherein Bill was to build a building for Doug for $100,000 and an additional on-time bonus of $10,000 if the building was completed on time. Doug is receiving the building in exchange for the money and Bill is receiving the money in exchange for the service.

Therefore, there is valid consideration and a valid contract has been formed.

CONDITIONS

An act or event not certain to occur, which if excused or satisfied, gives rise to or extinguishes a duty to perform under the terms of the contract.

Express Condition Precedent

In order to receive the $10,000 bonus, Bill must complete the project on time. Bill must fully satisfy the condition to receive this money.

Satisfaction of Condition

Bill failed to satisfy this condition due to the breach caused by Ellen. Substantial satisfaction is not adequate.

Excuse

Bill does not have a valid excuse. Doug does not owe Bill the bonus.

FORMATION OF CONTRACT 2

Supra.

Facts state that Bill subsequently entered into a valid contract with Ellen. Ellen was to perform the electrical work as a subcontractor for Bill for the price of $15,000. Bill is receiving Ellen's services in exchange for the money. Ellen is receiving the money in exchange for her labor for Bill's project.

Therefore, there is a valid consideration and valid contract has been formed.

THIRD PARTY RIGHTS

A contract in which the parties, at the time of the agreement, specifically intend to benefit a third party.

Privity

Doug is not in privity with Ellen because he is not a party to the contract. However, the privity requirement has been abolished under Lawrence v. Fox.

Intended Beneficiary

Doug will argue that he is an intended beneficiary of the Bill/Ellen contract because the work that was to be performed was for him.

However, Ellen will argue that Doug was not an intended beneficiary because she did not enter into the contract in order to benefit Doug, but only to gain employment from Bill. Ellen could have entered into a contract to work as a subcontractor for Bill for any number of projects which Bill may have been working. Her agreement with Bill does not mean that Ellen had a specific intent to benefit the client for whom Bill was contracted.

Therefore, Doug is not an intended beneficiary.

Creditor/Donee Beneficiary

If for some reason Doug can prove to the court that he is an intended beneficiary, the argument will continue as follows.

If Doug is an intended beneficiary, he is a creditor beneficiary because he is owed something under the Doug/Bill contract. Bill and Ellen are not performing their services in order to confer a gift upon Doug, but are doing so in exchange for the money Doug will pay. However, as discussed supra Doug is not likely an intended beneficiary.

Vesting

Doug does not have rights.

Defenses

None

Therefore, Doug will not be able to recover damages from Ellen for the late completion of the contract because he is not a party to the Bill/Ellen contract and is not an intended beneficiary.

Remedies/Damages

If Doug recovers at all, he will be able to recover from Bill for damages incurred due to Bill's failure to complete the project on time. Doug will be able to deduct his damages from the contract price. Bill will then be able to recover those damages from Ellen for her breach. See infra.

2. IS ELLEN LIABLE TO BILL FOR: THE LOSS OF THE ON-TIME BONUS? FOR ANY OTHER DAMAGES?

BILL V. ELLEN

FORMATION OF CONTRACT 2

Supra.

Facts state that Bill subsequently entered into a valid contract with Ellen. Ellen was to perform the electrical work as a subcontractor for Bill for the price of $15,000. Bill is receiving Ellen's services in exchange for the money. Ellen is receiving the money in exchange for her labor for Bill's project.

Therefore, there is a valid consideration and valid contract has been formed.

CONDITIONS

An act or event not certain to occur, which if excused or satisfied, gives rise to or extinguishes a duty to perform under the terms of the contract.

Constructive Condition Precedent

Generally, the longer performance must precede the shorter performance. Thus, Ellen has a duty to perform before receiving payment. However, in this case Ellen was receiving progress payments during the course of her performance.

DUTIES

Ellen had a duty to perform under the contract at the agreed upon price of $15,000. Bill had been paying her progress payments throughout the course of her performance. Thus, Ellen has no legal excuse for repudiating the contract and quitting.

Therefore, Ellen had a duty to perform.

BREACH

An unjustified failure to tender performance under the terms of the contract.

Ellen is in breach because she repudiated the contract and quit. Bill will argue that this is a major breach because her performance goes to the essence of her contract with Bill.

Therefore, Ellen's failure to perform is a breach of contract.

REMEDIES

General Damages - Expectation

Bill will be able to recover his expectation damages under the Bill/Ellen contract in order to put Bill back into the position he would have been in had the contract been performed by Ellen. Bill paid Ellen $3,000 for the work she had completed. Bill then had to pay Roger $20,000 to complete Ellen's work. Bill's total expense for the electrical work was $23,000. Bill will be able to recover the difference between the difference between his cost of covering for Ellen's breach and contract price agreed to with Ellen.

Therefore, Bill will be able to recover $8,000 from Ellen in expectation damages.

Special Damages - Consequential - Hadley v. Baxendale

Bill will try to recover his $10,000 bonus from Ellen because the project was not completed on time solely due to Ellen's breach. Under Hadley v. Baxendale, recovery of damages is limited to the foreseeable costs of breach. The facts state that at the time that Bill entered into his contract with Ellen that Ellen was unaware of Bill's on-time bonus. Because Ellen was unaware of the bonus, she had no reason to know of the lost profits that Bill would suffer if she breached the contract.

Therefore, since Ellen could not foresee the loss of $10,000 in profit to Bill at the time of the formation of her contract with Bill, the $10,000 will not be recovered by Bill.

Incidental Damages

Bill will be able to recover incidental expenses incurred in the course of trying to find a replacement for Ellen and to bring suit against her for breach.

Bill will also be able to recover damages incurred by Doug as a result of Bill's failure to complete the project on time. As discussed supra, Doug will be able to deduct his damages due to Bill's late completion from Bill. Bill will be able to pass those expenses on to Ellen.

QUESTION 4: SELECTED ANSWER B

1. IS ELLEN LIABLE FOR ANY DAMAGES DOUG MAY HAVE INCURRED AS A RESULT OF THE LATE COMPLETION.

THIRD PARTY CONTRACT

A third party contract is one that is intended to benefit a party other than the promissor and promisee and is made at contract formation.

PRIVITY

In a third party contract, a party must be a vested, intended beneficiary in order to enforce the contract.

INTENT TO BENEFIT

It must be shown that the contracting parties intended for the third party to benefit from the contract when it was formed.

Here there is nothing in the contract between Ellen and Bill to indicate that there was an intent to benefit Doug.

VESTING

An intended beneficiary's interest vests when they learn about the contract and assent to it.

An intended beneficiary may enforce a third party contract when their interests become vested.

DONEE OR CREDITOR BENEFICIARY OR INCIDENTAL BENEFICIARY

A donee beneficiary is one that receives benefit of the contract as a gift; a creditor beneficiary receives the benefit to satisfy an obligation due him by the promisee. An incidental beneficiary is one that will benefit from the contract but is not an intended beneficiary.

Doug would be an incidental beneficiary of the Bill/Ellen contract and would not have standing to enforce or recover under it.

CONCLUSION

There was no enforceable agreement between Doug and Bill that would allow him to recover.

2. IS ELLEN LIABLE TO BILL

WHAT LAW GOVERNS THE CONTRACT?

This is a contract building services and will be governed by the rules of the common law because it is not a contract for the sale of goods.

CONTRACT

A contract is an agreement between two [or] more parties the law will enforce. To be valid it must contain an offer, acceptance and consideration.

The facts indicate that there was a valid contract present between Doug and Bill and that contract contained a specified time of completion and an on-time bonus.

There was also a valid contract between Bill and Ellen for the electrical work to be done for $15,000.

STATUTE OF FRAUDS SATISFIED?

Under the common law certain contracts have to be in writing to be enforceable. These include contracts in consideration of marriage, those that cannot be completed in less than a year, executor guarantees and suretyship or those dealing with real property.

It's unclear if this contract is in writing, but because it can be completed in a year and is for a building not an interest in land it would not need to be in writing.

It appears the Statute of Frauds is satisfied.

DISCHARGE OF DUTY

A party's duty may be discharged if they have a valid excuse.

IMPOSSIBILITY

If it becomes objectively impossible for anyone to perform the duties under the contract, the defendant's duty may be discharged.

Ellen will claim that it is impossible for her to perform because she could not profitably do the electrical work for $15,000. This is not a valid excuse because someone else could do the work.

FRUSTRATON OF PURPOSE

When both parties know at the time of contract formation of a specific reason for the contract and the nonoccurrence of an event that was to occur happens and then the basis for the bargain is destroyed excusing the party from performance.

Here Ellen will claim that the purpose for her taking the contract was to turn a profit and when she couldn't do that her purpose in entering into the contract was frustrated.

This is an error in judgment, not a happening the nonoccurrence of would destroy the bargained-for exchange.

Frustration of purpose is not a valid defense.

COMMERCIAL IMPRACTICABILITY

When there is extreme and disproportionate disparity in the expense or effort in performance that was not part of the original agreement, the defendant may claim extreme financial hardship. The 10x rule is generally applied to see if completion of the agreement would cost the defendant ten times more than agreed. If so performance may be excused.

Commercial impracticability will fail because another contractor completed the electrical work for $20,000, which is not ten times the agreed upon price.

There do not appear to be any valid events that would discharge Ellen's duty to perform.

BREACH OF CONTRACT

A breach is the failure to perform one's absolute duty when it comes due.

Ellen failed to perform her duty because she quit after receiving $3000 in progress payments.

IS THE BREACH MAJOR OR MINOR

This would be a major breach because it severely impacted the bargained-for exchange when Ellen quit after completing only one-third of the work.

REMEDIES
DAMAGES - MONETARY AWARD FOR THE LOSS OF THE BENEFIT OF THE BARGAIN

a. THE LOSS OF THE ON-TIME BONUS
CONSEQUENTIAL DAMAGES

Under Hadley vs Baxendale consequential damages may be awarded for those damages that result from the failure of a contract. These must be contemplated by the parties at the time of formation, be clearly caused by the breach, be certain in amount, and could not have been avoided.

Here Bill will contend that the loss of the on-time bonus was solely caused by Ellen's quitting the job, as the facts indicate; so the loss was clearly caused by the breach by Ellen. The amount was certain because the on-time bonus was stated in the Doug/Bill contract to be $10,000. Bill will also argue that the loss could not have been avoided because he put forth his best efforts, but could not complete the work in time. On the other hand Ellen will argue that she had no idea of the on-time bonus when she entered into the agreement with Bill. The facts state Ellen was not aware of Bill's on-time bonus; therefore the loss by Bill was not contemplated by both parties at the time of formation. Ellen will further argue that she didn't learn about the bonus until before she began the job.

It appears that Ellen will have the stronger argument.

CONCLUSION

The fact that Ellen did not know about the on-time bonus at the time the contract was formed will most likely preclude Bill from recovering that amount from her.

b. FOR ANY OTHER DAMAGES

EXPECTATION DAMAGES

Expectation damages are to recover the benefit of the bargain for the non-breaching party.

Bill should be able to recover the difference between what he had to pay Roger, $20,000, and the contract price of the original contract $15,000, or $5,000. He may be able to recover the additional $3000 that Ellen received in progress payments, if he can show that the work was one-third complete and the cost to finish was an additional $20,000. If that is the case, Bill should be able to recover $8000 from Ellen.